Advance Praise for
"The Bear Facts of Life"

"Dr. McLaughlin is a gifted communicator with the unique ability to share ideas that will add value to anyone's journey in both business and life"
—Kevin Brown, *The HERO Effect*

"As a writer and publisher, I've read my fair share of books. Rarely do the words evoke a strong emotional response from me. This is the exception.
Patrick's wisdom and heartfelt message will resonate deep into the hearts of nearly anyone. It's a book I would be proud to put on my shelf, but more valuable in the hands of my children."
—Doug Crowe, Author Your Brand, Inc.

"The Bear Facts of Life is filled with important lessons about how to live your best life. Pat captures the essence of joy, loyalty, and unconditional love that dogs bring into our homes and hearts. This book is a treasure trove of wisdom and emotions that resonate deeply, reminding us to cherish every moment with our beloved pets, and to exemplify their best traits when engaging with others."
—Steve Hockett, CEO,
Rob Goggins, President
Great Clips

The Bear Facts of Life: How My Dog Showed Me How to Live

by Patrick McLaughlin

Published in the United States by Payton-Parker Publishing

ISBN: 9798330221875

Book design by Diana Wade

Dedication

I dedicate this book to all dog owners. By observing and listening to your furry friend, the secrets to a well lived life are at the end of the leash.

I dedicate this book to those needing a positive boost in their life. I hope you will find this short read to be uplifting to your spirit.

And I dedicate this book to Bear, my favorite dog!

To all, Be A Bear!

I've had nine dogs in my life. Their names are easy to remember. The first four started with the letter M, and the last five started with the letter B.

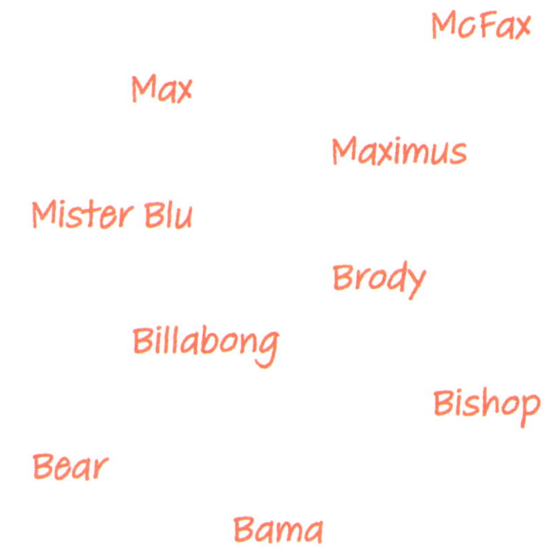

There was no reason behind this, we just kept the same initials.

The breeds were:

German shepherd

Dalmatian

Great Dane

Three miniature poodles

Three goldendoodles

In that order.

My wife had always believed in having two dogs (or more), so that each dog could have a companion and playmate when we were away. This is the main reason I've had so many dogs in my later life.

Of all these dogs, my favorite is Bear.

I know that as parents we're not supposed to have favorites, but maybe pet parents have a pass, because they're not blood related, and picking dogs from a litter or a rescue organization can be a hit-or-miss situation. You never truly know how their personalities are going to develop and how they're going to fit in with the family until you've brought them home, integrate them with your family, attempt to train them and they start to grow.

Bear's specifics:

Weight: 94 pounds

Color: Black

Gender: Male

Breed: Goldendoodle

Personality: Goofy, Loving, Friendly, Mild-mannered.

Like most dogs, he has a plethora of nicknames:

Bob.

Baba.

And my favorite: Big Bad Bobby Bear.

In Bear's litter, there were ten dogs. Bear was the only male and one of three black ones while the other seven were a retriever tan color. He was the absolute biggest in the litter. We wanted a big dog, and he looked like a little black baby bear. He was black like his soon-to-be brother, Bishop.

Why did Bear become my favorite? Well, the following pages will tell you why. He is an inspiration to me in so many ways, and by observing him, he's exemplified to me in so many ways how to live a better life. Bear taught me a lot about what it means to really, truly live a full life.

It's been said that if a dog could do one thing a human could do on this Earth, it would be to speak. And it's my belief that if a human being could do one thing a dog could do on this Earth, it would be to always live in the present.

I

The First Bear Fact of Life:
Be Present

I have two different jobs that require two totally different skill sets. On the days when I work as a chiropractor, I am on my feet all day, seeing over one hundred patients between 6:45 a.m. and 6:00 p.m. This leaves me mentally and physically exhausted. On the days when I work as a franchise owner of Great Clips hair salons, I sit in meetings, navigating the businesses and 400 plus employees.

At either job, it's a long day, and I look forward to coming home to my wife and dogs.

When I pulled into the driveway, I would see the silhouette of my Bear through the glass front door.

Sitting. Waiting...

When he had seen me emerge from the car door, he howled so loudly, I could hear him through the closed door. He jumped up and down, his tail wagging a mile a minute, greeting me as if it had been years since he saw me, not hours. He greeted me as if I've just done something spectacular, like gone to the moon and back or saved a dozen people from a horrible death. While I consider what I do important and a privilege, it's not deserving of the enthusiasm Bear gave me.

I struggled to open the door because of his counter pressure on the other side, and once I finally pushed through, it was an all-out love assault on me. Jumping, kissing, sniffing, with his tail going a mile a minute. He truly was in the present while greeting me, using all his energy and enthusiasm just to say hello.

It was as if he were saying:

I missed you.

I am here with you now.

He was sometimes so over the top in his greeting that he knocked me down to the ground with his leaps and bounds.

This was one of the most comforting things Bear did for me. Yes, it's beyond what was necessary, but hey, who doesn't love being greeted like a hero at the end of a long workday?

Living in the present had always been a challenge for me, in all facets of my life. In my work as a chiropractor, I have to be present every visit of the day. It might be my sixtieth patient of the day, but it is that patient's first visit of the day. I must give them my full attention to help heal them.

Being a father of four, I wanted to be present with each of my kids when they were living at home, and now, when we visit or get on the phone. Being with them right here and right now is important, and not being tugged away with other thoughts or my phone.

As an owner of fifty hair salons, I bring my presence to work every day to be laser-focused on the tasks at hand: human resource issues, training, recruiting, handling corporate needs, visiting the businesses, and the meeting and tackling of challenges that surface over the course of a day with running different locations simultaneously.

Being present is a huge part of life. I feel regrets about the past mistakes I've made, and often have fear and anxieties about the uncertainties in life that lie ahead. But when I wallow in the past or worry about the future, I miss out on the only time that really matters: the time that we have now in front of us. The present—a gift in its most literal sense.

The Paw

Bear showed me he was present for me with his paw. He would sit down next to me, either while I was working at my desk or watching television on the couch, patiently staring at me, and then put his paw on my lap.

It was like he was saying:

Here I am . . . pay attention to me and be present.

He was always at my feet when I wrote and worked. Always there. Always present.

Dogs nudge us to cherish the present and find joy in simple moments. They stand in front of us, demanding attention with a paw on your lap, looking at us with love. "Put that phone down, look around you. It's a beautiful day—let's play."

Bear, with his over-the-top, knock-me-down greeting, taught me the importance of the present, each and every day.

He showed me that he was always there for me, and not just greeting me at the door, but sticking by my side.

Being present for humans is different, but equally important. Present-time consciousness is when you are with someone—*you are truly with someone*—and not thinking about other things. You can feel the difference when someone is focused on you, your thoughts and your feelings, and cares about what you're going through.

Bear, and all dogs when they're with you, are *with* you. This is the epitome of being present. Being present allows us to learn, adapt, and find joy, even amidst difficulties.

Especially when one puts his paw on you to be with them.

Live your own true life and live in the present as much as you possibly can.

As my kids have grown, as I have taken more on professionally and personally, and as more and more technology has reared its distracting head, I have found being present is more challenging than ever, with the most egregious object being the cell phone that is in almost every human's hand.

As I have aged, I have realized two things:

Being present is more difficult.

Being present has never been more important, for the time we have on Earth is finite.

Be present to enjoy all that life has to offer every day: the events, the blessings, and the people around us. When you are with a customer, be *with* the customer, not thinking about other things that are going on in your life.

The time we have is all we have, and not being present is a waste of this precious time.

Bear reminded me to be present daily.

Like a dog, learn to be present.

When you are serving your coworkers, be with them, and not thinking about other work challenges.

When you are at work, think about your present state and think about work, not personal issues.

When you are at home, think about being present with all you are around, not about work.

Yes, it's easier said than done. Being present is one of the hardest things that we do in life, because our mind is filled with regrets, second thoughts about the past, and worries and uncertainties of the future.

Be in the now with what you are doing and who you are with.

Bear did this better than any human.

While being present is a large reason for my success as a spouse, parent, and entrepreneur, it was my dog Bear that continued to show me that being present is what life is all about.

Like a dog, remind yourself to be present for those you're with.

If Bear could have spoken, he would have said to me, "Dad, look, this sunbeam is warm, and your lap is cozy. Let's just be here, together. Be present and live your life with me now. Don't be distracted by work or that TV. Here is my paw. Let's shake hands and be present together."

Translated further: Dogs remind us to look away from technology, stay present, greet each other with enthusiasm, and place our paws, or hands, on each other when needed.

A dog's effect on living fully: Live your own true life, and live in the present as much as you possibly can.

2

The Second Bear Fact of Life:
Be Loving

The Tail

Is there any better example of seeing love from a dog than the wag of its tail? Bear had a bushy, well-groomed tail, and it wildly wagged from side to side when he truly loved to see you.

Bear showed his love to me with his tail wagging every time he saw me. Sometimes he wagged his tail so vigorously he knocked things off the coffee table. His tongue was out, and he was panting in such a way to indicate that he wanted me to scratch his back and reciprocate this love back to him.

Authenticity in relationships leads to deeper connections, emotional fulfillment, and a richer life. Be loving always. Life is too short not to love one another. Love is what this world needs. Every person needs love every day.

Loving everyone is not the easiest thing to do in the world, of course. Sometimes I have rude patients who are tough to love. I have unhappy employees and customers in my other businesses. Obviously, kids can make love difficult at times with their actions and words. And if you have ever been married for a long period of time, always loving your spouse can sometimes be challenging too.

Loving yourself is always the biggest challenge of all. Loving yourself is the number one thing you need to do, because you cannot give away love to others if you don't have enough love stored inside.

Loving yourself. Loving your spouse. Loving your kids. Loving your friends. Loving your employees and coworkers. Loving your customers.

Love is critical to make this world go round.

There is no better embodiment of this than the love you can see in the dog who always loves.

Especially with his tail wagging.

Like a dog, learn to love.

When my entire family was around, Bear's heart was full, as was mine. We have four kids: two daughters and two sons. As they are all grown now and out of the house, there is no better blessing than when we are all together, which is unfortunately rare now because they live in different parts of the country. Our gatherings occur during the typical holiday times, and as we all gather in the family room on couches and loveseats, the dogs encourage us to celebrate our true selves and connect authentically.

Bear didn't care what we looked like, whether we were in our nice clothes or just sweatpants and T-shirts, with some of us more tired than others due to the late-night, cross-country travel. Bear would "work the room," going from one person to the next, greeting each of us individually by sitting in front of us and putting his paw on us. He was essentially saying, "I love you; can you please love me back?"

He'd patiently wait for:

his back to get scratched,

his head to get scratched,

his throat to get scratched,

his tummy to get rubbed,

and his ears to get rubbed.

Bear got plenty of scratches, rubs, and kisses in return for his loving looks and attention.

Bear was full of love, and it showed during these precious family gatherings.

It can be easy to love when all is going smoothly, but harder when there are bumps in the road. Sometimes, when I was in a bad mood and affected by something that had negatively impacted me, Bear simply did not care what my attitude was. He wanted to be present with me. He wanted to love me, no matter my attitude. And with him sitting in front of me with that goofy look on his face—

half-opened eyes and his tongue out, just staring at me—his unconditional love inevitably meant I couldn't stay grouchy for long.

I was fascinated by a book I read, *The Five Secrets You Must Discover Before You Die*. The author, John Izzo, interviewed 235 people over the age of sixty (with the oldest being 105).

Izzo discovered that all happy and wise people eventually discover and live these five secrets. One of these was to "Become Love," that is, become a loving person for others, and most importantly, love yourself.

Bear, even though he was not a human over sixty, knew this from birth.

Authenticity in relationships and self-expression leads to deeper connections, emotional fulfillment, and a richer life.

Accepting that we are perfectly human means that we are not perfect, and some-

times that is one of the most difficult things to accept in this life.

Loving yourself requires that you give yourself grace to be human.

Loving yourself also requires us to accept who we are to know that we are loved by others and God.

Like a dog, learn to be loving. Always.

If Bear could have spoken, he would have said to me, "I love you, even when you're grumpy or messy. You're you, I love you, and I love having you alongside me!"

Translated further: Dogs remind us to look past our own faults and the faults of others, and give our loving best.

A dog's effect on living fully: Love is the basis of all religions, and nothing exemplifies a dog's feeling toward their owner more than love. A dog's DNA is spelled L-O-V-E. Love is what makes this world work, and when one is giving love and accepting love, similar to a dog, life is full.

The Third Bear Fact of Life:
Be (Paws-itively) Happy

Life is too short not to be happy.

In The Five Thieves of Happiness, John Izzo wrote, "Psychology and spirituality have one important shared quest. They both seek to answer the question: *How do human beings find happiness and meaning?*"

He wrote that happiness is a "default mechanism" to each human being. We are born with this potential. It resides within us. It is natural.

However, Izzo found the five main "thieves" of happiness that, when allowed into our brains and hearts, will rob us of this default mechanism:

Control,

conceit,

coveting,

consumption,

comfort.

Interestingly, dogs have none of these.

They are never worried about control, perhaps because they have very little of it. They never seem to worry about where they go and what to do, who to be with and who they are going to play with. Dogs have very little control over their environments.

They are never worried about conceit. They don't worry about being the best dog in the world, the one who can jump the highest, or the smartest. They just are who they are.

They are never worried about coveting. (With the exception of when another dog has their bone, or when a human has delicious food!)

They are never worried about consumption. They don't have dreams of a bigger house or a softer bed or more toys. They are happy with a stick.

They are never worried about being too comfortable. They like a cool wooden or tile floor. Yes, they'd like to sleep on our beds, but understand if they can't and will still greet us with tails wagging if they have to sleep apart from us.

Thus, dogs are inherently happy. They don't worry too much about life, because they put their faith in us. Most responsible dog owners take excellent care of their dogs, and it's a mutually trusting and loving relationship.

Bear always had a happy look on his face. Mouth open. Tongue hanging out. Eyes half closed. I rubbed his chest all the time just to see his happy face.

Fetch

The number one thing that makes any goldendoodle happy is one word and one word only: *fetch*.

Or, as we said in our household, "You wanna play ball?"

Bear immediately went into hysterics, jumping up and down and running straight to the nearest door, anticipating what fun we'd have in this activity that made him the happiest.

Bear played with us in the yard until we said "quit." This was his happy zone, as it is in the DNA of all retrievers.

On one occasion, though, during the summer, we almost played too much ball with Big Bad Bobby Bear. I was talking with a neighbor at the same time as I was throwing the ball for my sweet boy, over and over again. Little did I realize that, like good conversations go, we kept talking on and on, and it lasted probably forty-five minutes.

In the eighty-five-degree heat.

With Bear wearing a full coat of fur.

And he fetched that ball 100 plus times without hesitation, ready to go another 100.

When I took him inside, and he got his water, he literally passed out.

Bear lied on the ground in the kitchen, and his eyes rolled back in his head.

My wife immediately called the vet in a panic, while I lied down with the dog, trying to shake him awake.

The vet told us to cool him down immediately in a bathtub. We scooped him up and put him in a tub and turned on the cold water. My wife went and got a bowl of ice and immersed it in the tub to help revive him and cool him off. Within a minute or so, Bear was conscious and back on his feet.

It had been a very close call.

I hate to admit it, but it was totally my

fault, and we were so lucky he survived.

Bear had not cared how hot he was, though, because he was in his happy zone.

It was my stupidity in not recognizing the health risk of running a ninety-pound dog on nonstop thirty-and forty-yard sprints, in eighty-five-degree weather while wearing a fur jacket.

Lesson learned.

However, this epitomized how focused on happiness Bear was with this activity. He was in his zone. (While I should have been as equally present with him as I had been with my neighbor I was chatting with.)

He loved fetching more than anything else in life.

This made him happy and put him in a positive mood.

Happiness Is Found with Curiosity

Dogs inspire us to follow our curiosity, seeking joy in unexpected places. Bear was curious and wanted to meet and greet everyone. Almost too much so. One bad habit he had is that he would literally jump on every stranger, lovingly that is, to try to lick their face. This was too much for some, but Bear loved to greet everyone with this exuberant, and curious, loving way.

Dogs remind us to be curious and to look at all opportunities in life. To bask in the beauty of God's creation by noticing all that is around us. After all, *dog* is *God* spelled backward. Being curious brings out the inquisitive child inside all of us who wonder at everything and is always asking questions. Being curious is a part of living a great life and feeling alive.

A dog shows us how important it is to explore new places, be curious about what's happening in the world, and learn more.

Unlike dogs, we humans can use our gift of speech to ask people questions. This sense of wonder and joy enriches our lives, making our years more vibrant and fulfilling.

Attitude is everything in life, and being positive and happy is a choice we all have. In *The Positive Dog* by Jon Gordon, he writes that we have two "dogs" inside us, one positive and one negative. The one that speaks the loudest is "the one that you feed."

Being negative spurs more negativity, while being positive encourages more positivity. Having a positive and happy attitude is a choice, and many people fail to see this. They just blame their circumstances and never realize it's the way they see life that makes them happy. Being positive in my chiropractic practice has led me to have long-standing employees and patients alike.

Being positive in my businesses presented me with trusted employees and return customers.

Being encouraging and positive is a choice I make as an employer. Although I am human and can fall into the negativity trap from time to time, I choose to be as positive as possible to help encourage my coworkers, employees, customers, and patients.

This starts with a smile and an approachable, positive, encouraging demeanor and attitude.

As my parents taught me, "Praise in public and discipline in private." This fosters great employee relationships and allows constructive feedback to be shared in a positive light.

Positivity is a choice.

The Losada Line is an important measure for dealing with people and relationships. It says that when you give at least three positive compliments to one constructive critique, this sets the table for a positive relationship. A 3:1 ratio of being positive to negative is critical for fostering relationships. Unfortunately, a lot of us are in the 1:1 ratio here, and this affects those we relate to.

But being positive is a choice and a practice that has helped me govern my businesses and the relationships around me.

Being positive as a father has led to a strong family bond where my kids want to go through the hassle of flying or driving home on holiday weekends to be with their mother and me.

I refuse to let bad days get me down, or worse, bring others down with me.

Being negative is an attitudinal choice just as being positive is. In *Man's Search for*

Meaning, Viktor Frankl states that this is the one thing that we have control over: our attitude.

Being negative around family can lead to a ruined meal or an upsetting gathering.

Being negative at work can be contagious as well, for I find negativity will spread more rampantly in the workplace than positivity.

In dealing with customers and other businesses, it is said if you do a good job, people will tell one other person. When you don't meet a customer's needs, they will tell eleven people.

A negative attitude can ruin family relationships, businesses, and customer relationships.

The positive and happy side of my dog, Bear, serves as a constant reminder that this is the attitude that I need to manifest in my life and remain as positive as I can at all times. I do not have time for "stinking thinking," and Bear is the constant reminder for me to always put a smile on my face.

Like a dog, learn to be positively happy.

If Bear could have spoken, he would have said to me, "Let's explore—behind that tree, under those leaves. Oh, that scent! It's like a thousand stories! Life's full of surprises and joy and happiness. Happiness is within you. You have to find it."

Translated further: Dogs remind us to sniff out our own happiness and wag our tail about it. Happiness is a choice, and when we look closely at our lives, there is so much to be thankful and happy about. If we will only look!

A dog's effect on living fully: There is a positive and negative dog residing within us. The one that rears its head is the one that we feed. Being positively happy is an attitudinal choice that we all have. Being "paws-itively" happy is a universal dog trait that is worth emulating each day.

4

The Fourth Bear Fact of Life:
Be Loyal

Bear's second favorite activity, after playing ball, was to take a long walk with anyone in the family. Our favorite spots were in the neighborhood, downtown Nashville, Tennessee (he loved to visit The Parthenon); downtown Morehead City, North Carolina; or at the ocean at Atlantic Beach, North Carolina.

Just grabbing the leash and saying, "You wanna take a walk?" produced the same amount of exuberance as fetch. Jumping, twirling, tail wagging as fast as possible, panting, mouth wide open in a grin.

On a walk, it's easy to sense a dog's loyalty. We are lucky to live near the beach, and on our wet and sandy walks, Bear stayed right by my side. Proud to be walking with me, ears perked up, on alert to protect me from any predators, but also delighting in the exercise and adventure. After a few minutes of him tugging me, he calmed down, relaxing into his human's pace.

He barked at dogs passing by and other people, loyally protecting me, like a furry bodyguard.

Nothing would be a more loyal act than Bear just being by my side for a long, one-hour walk in the park. Bear walked faithfully by my side, just as a friend would, but he was also saying with his proud posture: *Look at my dad, he's taking me for a walk!* There was a rhythm to our walks, step by step by step. He loved being next to me on a walk.

Lying Down

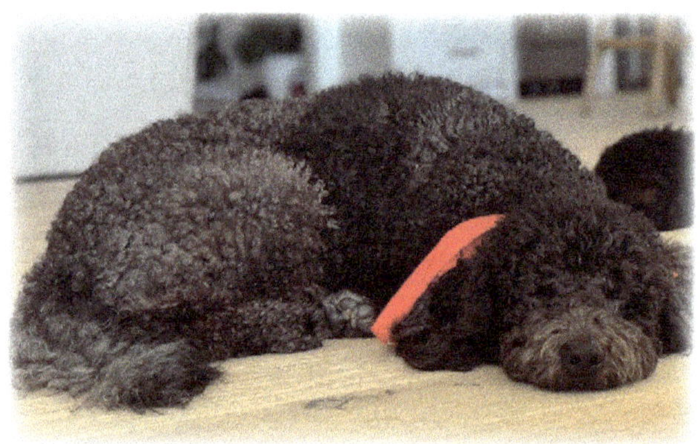

Is there any better example of a dog's loyalty than them being in the room with you all day? As much as they want to be outside, they'll stick by you as you sit at your boring old desk.

I work at home a considerable amount of time, and Bear just loved to be next to me. Everywhere. Whether in my office, watching television, or in my bedroom, when he plopped down right next to me, it was like he was saying, "Dad, I'm here for you if you need me." While I wrote, he loved to lie down right on my feet as I punched away at the keys.

It was a great comfort to know I had a loyal friend who was always there for me.

One of the most meaningful books I've read was Viktor Frankl's *Man's Search for Meaning*, in which he writes about his horrific experiences in Nazi concentration camps during World War II. He was separated from his wife and family, and his handwritten manuscript—his life's work—had been discovered and destroyed.

Frankl's goal became to reunite with his family and rewrite his book, and this desire kept him alive. This was his North Star.

But for some of his fellow prisoners, apathy took over. He noted how a large portion of prisoners died shortly after the holidays every year when they lost all hope that they were going to be freed from the atrocities of their concentration camp.

Frankl's hope for a meaningful future and his loyalty to the idea that he needed to rewrite his work and be reunited with his family are what kept him alive. He also made sure to convene with other people who had the same hopes and desires to remain alive.

His ultimate survival, after being sent to four concentration camps, demonstrates how a hopeful attitude is the one thing that can never be taken away from you.

Bear reminded me of this in far less stressful circumstances; nevertheless, he showed how hope and loyalty are linked together.

Like lying down next to me all day long, his loyalty to me was there. I was the most important thing to him in the world, no matter what I was doing. Playing ball, going on walks, or sitting in front of a boring computer. He didn't care. He just wanted to be by my side. And he remained hopeful that, after a while, we'd eventually do something more fun.

Loyalty is huge to me. Loyalty means being there no matter what. Loyalty is earned with time and trust. Loyalty, like trust, is earned drip by drip, but can be lost in buckets.

Employees demonstrate loyalty by showing up at work on time and doing their job. As a business owner, I earn employees' loyalty by providing a good business environment that is growth-based and consistently excellent.

As a chiropractic physician, I earn patient loyalty by giving them a comfortable, inviting environment where they feel safe and cared for. I also earn their loyalty by giving them the best results possible, as well as by referring them out when we are not getting the results that we were both expecting.

Creating loyalty as a parent means mentoring my adult kids when they need it the most. Creating loyalty for my wife is simply being there for her when she needs my support. As the marriage vows state, being there in good times and bad, and in sickness and health helps create loyalty for both of us. Bear exemplified loyalty every day. Life is better lived with loyalty. Dogs remind us of that.

Like a dog, remind yourself to be loyal to those you love.

If Bear could have spoken, he would have said to me, "Rain or shine, I'm by your side. You're my pack, my heart. Loyalty isn't a choice; it's who I am. It is my attitude."

Translated further: Dogs remind us to stand by those we love, unwavering and true.

A dog's effect on living fully: Loyal connections provide emotional support, resilience, and a sense of purpose. They contribute to a more meaningful and complete life. Attitude is everything.

5

The Fifth Bear Fact of Life:
Chase Experiences

As a half golden retriever, Bear loved to chase whatever you threw for him. He loved to go to the end of the dock with me every morning. He loved a walk on the beach. He loved to play with his brothers and sister in the backyard. He loved boat trips.

We lived in Nashville, Tennessee, for three years with Bear. One morning, Bear trotted down a hill to the lake's edge. The next thing I saw, twenty deer flew right past me with Bear at their tails, running after them as fast as he could. It took us about thirty minutes to find Bear, because he was so determined to catch a deer, which, of course, he didn't, and we were grateful.

He slept for about four solid hours when we finally got him back to the house.

Another experience he chased was when I played golf on our local course. I was on the green and looked up, and there was Bear! He was out on the golf course, just wandering around. Apparently, the door of our home had not been fully closed, and Bear was walking around, taking it all in, like he wished he could grab a club and play eighteen holes. I grabbed him and put him in the golf cart and took him back home.

One time at our dock in Morehead City, Bear and I were walking back from the boat, which was docked at the end of the pier. I had my arms full of stuff I needed to take back to the house. As we walked side by side, I accidentally dropped a beach chair, which startled Bear enough that he jumped off the side of the dock and landed in the water. With 300 feet to shore, Bear navigated himself to the shore safely. He didn't swim often, but when he did, he swam effortlessly.

Being on the dock with chairs crashing versus having a nice dive and swim? Bear chose the more adventurous experience.

Dogs urge us to prioritize moments over tasks, to chase our passions with fervor.

An impactful book and video for me and many others, Randy Pausch's *The Last Lecture* has been seen by millions on YouTube. It was given just after he was told he had a few months to live.

The lecture was not so much about dying—it was about living.

Pausch said he knew he had a great childhood because he couldn't find any pictures of himself as a kid where he wasn't smiling.

In the lecture, Pausch states that when you do the right thing, good stuff has a way of happening. In essence, Pausch focuses on chasing life's experiences versus chasing material things.

As I get older, it is the experiences of life that mean the most to me, certainly not things. Experiences with the kids and my wife over the years—at home or on a ball field or on vacation—are the most cherished parts of my life. We live in a world hyper-focused on material possessions, and we are missing experiences. The older I get, this is what I will continue to aim for: chase experiences as enthusiastically as Bear chasing a ball or herding deer. The right experiences will reward you with memories for a lifetime. It has for me.

Like a dog, learn to chase experiences versus accumulating things.

If Bear could have spoken, he would have said to me, "Dad, look up! The sky's on fire. Forget emails and deadlines. Let's chase colors, breathe, and feel alive!"

Translated further: Dogs remind us that life is full of rich experiences. We need to be ready for these opportunities and go for it.

A dog's effect on living fully: Prioritizing moments over tasks, pursuing passions, and embracing life's colors—lush green grass, Carolina blue skies and waters, majestic white snow, and multicolored sunrises and sunsets—lead to a more fulfilled existence.

6

The Sixth Bear Fact of Life:
Live Every Day to the Fullest

Tim McGraw wrote and recorded a famous song, "Live Like You Were Dying." No one knows but our maker when our time on this Earth will be up.

Each day is defined by the 1,440 minutes within. You cannot get them back. How many times in jest do you say, knowing that you have just wasted some of this precious time, "Boy, I will never get those ten minutes back."

My old JV football coach's favorite last line before every game was, "Play it like it's your last one." He was right. I played for him for two years, and, of course, with playing football came injuries, sidelining players, sometimes for the season. Their stories would become the motivational examples for the entire year. "Look at so and so—he is done for the year. What would he do for one more game? One more play?" The melodrama was there in every game.

This is true in so much of life. As a chiropractor, I try to help people heal so that they can resume the activities they enjoy: bicycling, running, basketball, or even returning to just walking normally. We don't realize until an injury what a privilege it is to be active, travel, and not to be in pain when lifting a baby or working in the garden.

How many times when you were at a funeral did you think: What wouldn't this person do to be here today with us? Funerals give you the ultimate perspective: life on Earth ends, and we never know when it's coming. One day it will be us. It is this perspective that makes living in the present that much more important.

When we are not living each day to the maximum, we are wasting the precious little time that we have on this planet. After my grandfather died, I was talking to an older friend of mine who shared a wise quote. He said, "When you are dead, you are dead for a very, very long time." I stopped to think about that for a minute and it grabbed me. Correct: you are dead forever.

Live hard every day to the best of your ability, because you just have the one life, and the clock is ticking. Make sure that you are living every day like it is the most important day you have. Because it is. When I focus on this reality, that each day is a precious gift, I am a better husband, father, chiropractor, business owner, and friend. I'm living in the moment and making the most out of my day.

Reading *Four Thousand Weeks*, by Oliver Burkeman, really brought home to me the preciousness of time. According to Google, the average life expectancy in the world is 79.25 years of age. Burkeman's book predicts that most people have an average of 4,000 weeks if they live to this age.

Life is finite.

There are no guarantees we will meet the average.

I was so moved and shaken by this realization that I put a countdown app on my phone that has the 4,000 weeks of my own life. Using this app, I get a continuous life countdown in years, months, weeks, days, hours, minutes, and even seconds. You cannot get time back. Time is ticking.

Life is indeterminate in that none of us know our last day on this Earth.

Life is finite as Burkeman points out. Some get more, and an unfortunate few get a lot less.

It is time to live.

Most goldendoodles live about twelve years. Bear's lifespan was set to be about 600 weeks. We know on an intellectual basis that dogs don't live as long as humans, and we age our dogs by giving them seven years of life for every human year.

One day in October, on a Sunday, it was a beautiful fall day with a chill in the air. Sunny. Carolina-blue skies. Just a textbook gorgeous day to be alive.

As was typical for me, at 7:30 in the morning, I walked my dogs to the end of the dock to meditate. I use that time to think and pray about many things in my life. However, that day, I'd just recently gotten Wi-Fi on the dock, and had a TV installed for fun times on the dock to watch sports. So instead of being quiet and meditative, I turned on ESPN's SportsCenter that morning, and caught up on my favorite sport, college football. I also brought a book out there as well if I got bored. I typically like to be out there for about an hour on Sunday mornings.

Boats moved up and down the Intercoastal Waterway that morning, providing some wake along the end of the dock. I sighed with the appreciation of these beautiful views, my wonderful life, the privilege of getting to watch a TV show on the dock, and having Bear by my side.

Bear was the only dog I had that would go back home on the 394-foot dock by himself. This is the length of a football field, from endzone to endzone. The other dogs would wait for me to go back to the house and walk by my side, but Bear had the courage to freelance by himself and walk back solo. He did it all the time, and my wife would simply let him in the house while she made coffee.

There were two unusual things that that morning. First, I usually would catch a glimpse of him walking midway back down the pier, or catch him on the lawn or by the door. But I didn't that morning, and my sixth sense said to me, *boy he got back quick.* The second unusual thing was that I stayed out there thirty minutes longer watching *SportsCenter.* Typically, my wife would have let him back out, and he would have rejoined me by the time I walked back.

Bear liked to check on me.

I finally went back home with the other two dogs, Bishop, another eighty-five-pound goldendoodle, and Billabong, a twenty-pound miniature poodle.

As I went back inside the house, I still could not find Bear. I hurried into my bedroom and my wife was in the room, with no Bear.

Hmm.

I hurried up the stairs to see if my son, who was home from college, had him in his room. He was still asleep, with no Bear.

I then rushed to the front yard. Maybe he was there? Nope.

My head started spinning. I ran to the start of the dock, thinking he must be asleep at the end of the dock . . . which would be a first.

And as I got to the beginning of the pier to go to the end of the dock, there he was.

Waves crashed over him. The sun still beaming beautifully, despite this terrible sight.

There was Bear.

With a white frothy mouth.

Drowned.

Dead.

I leaped over the bulkhead to get him, tearing my feet to shreds on oyster shells.

I picked up my lifeless dog and carried him to the edge of the bulkhead.

My favorite dog I ever had suddenly died.

Bear was gone.

Bear had started having seizures a few months prior to this. They were vicious: his eyes rolled back in his head, his mouth became frothy, and uncontrolled spasms wracked his body.

He had these about once a month, and they scared the dickens out of me.

My biggest fear was realized: he had a seizure on the dock, fell in the water and drowned.

A wave of guilt broke over me. Why did I not see him or hear him fall in?

I cried more than I ever had in my entire life for the next two months. I was inconsolable at times.

For those of you who have had sudden, unexpected tragedies with your human loved ones, I cannot imagine your pain or your loss. Because this hit so hard, I can't fathom the pain and grief of losing a spouse or a child. Bear was just a dog.

Why did it pain me so much that he was gone?

As I shared this with others, they reminded me that Bear was not "just a dog," but a big part of my family.

I meditated on this, and realized that this was so true, as I'd spent hours and hours with this animal every day. More so than my grown kids, and parents, and other relatives and friends.

Bear taught me on his last day:

It was for him.

In the end, I understand now why some people choose not to have dogs. Because of dogs' short lifespans, putting a dog down or watching a dog die is just too much for the heart to endure. People anticipate this grief, and it keeps them from joining the dog-own-ing world, for they know that they will outlive this furry companion.

Life is short, and dogs Bear's size live about 600 weeks. Unfortunately, Bear only lived about 300 weeks. Life is finite in time and indeterminate in not knowing when our last day will be.

Bear's sudden death put me in a life spiral of, first, guilt that I was the last person to be with him. Why did I not hear him splash? Why was I not more attentive to watch him go back on the pier, especially knowing his recent history of seizures? This caused many sleepless nights. His death was humbling for me in that I realized more in his demise that I was simply human.

I now understand the common saying that "tomorrow is never promised." After diving into a few months of depression after his death, I climbed out of it to find myself more focused on the meaningful parts of life. The experiences of being present with others. Spending time around people I truly love. Being as happy as I can be and doing the things that bring me true joy. Being loyal. Going after experiences in life that create memories with my loved ones. And last but not least, attempting to live life more fully, not taking the day or the moment for granted, and living each day like it could be the last.

All dogs possess these six traits.

I heard a sermon once where the preacher stated that as humans, we aspire to be like dogs because their purposeful intuition is set at birth. Think about it. Retrievers retrieve. Bloodhounds smell. Shepherds protect. Greyhounds run fast.

Dogs are additionally born with this innate DNA of presence, love, happiness, loyalty, experience-based living, and a zest to live a full life every single day.

For humans, it may take a lifetime for us to figure out the value in living with these traits, and sadly, some of us never will. The beauty of a dog is that if observed, they remind us of these traits daily.

Bear's death was a reminder to my family that life is not to be taken for granted. Predictably, there will be a day when my wife and I will be gone, and our kids will have to cope with feelings similar to how we feel now with Bear's passing. Conversations with my kids have been more poignant with the realization that life is to be lived day to day, and that we need to embrace each one of our gatherings that much more.

Bear's death has really hurt me. I miss his goofy, affable self. I miss him sitting next to me with his paw on me. I miss his great bark and just the feel of his mane when I put my hands through it, petting that large, fluffy animal. I miss his presence and the constant love he always showed me. He wasn't just a pet; he was my friend, and a treasured part of my family. He was a part of my life.

I miss him.

I miss his personality.

I miss his presence.

I miss Bear.

My favorite dog.

Postscript

During Christmas break of that year, my family gathered around our firepit to have a memorial service for Bear. We all told stories about what he meant to us. Bear lived six years and he left us with six powerful facts of life. The themes of being present, being loving, being loyal, being happy, chasing what life has to offer, and living life fully, like it is your last day, resonated through the service.

At the end, all six of us walked to the end of the dock that night with a full moon over us. We divvied up Bear's ashes in six small bowls, and we peered into the moonlit sound in front of us. We were at the site of Bear's last breath on the end of our dock. In unison, we all tossed Bear's ashes in the water.

It might have been my imagination, however, as the ashes were swimming on top of the sound, I could see the image of a large, black goldendoodle in my tear-filled eyes drifting away from me in the beautiful, picturesque evening.

Bear was with us that night.

And with how he reminded us how to live, he is still with us every day.

Post-Postscript

As devastated as my wife and I were with the passing of Bear, and against the advice of multiple people and many online resources, we did what we shouldn't have done according to the experts.

Within two months of Bear's passing, we added another furry pet to our family.

Another goldendoodle.

Unlike Bear, he is white.

Born in Alabama, we named him Bama.

Like a mother who goes through the amnesia of not remembering the sleepless nights and the efforts needed to raise a newborn, we fell into this trap as well with our new two-month-old puppy.

There was no replacing Bear, we knew that.

However, we do know that the pros heavily outweigh the cons for us when it comes to dog ownership, and we couldn't help ourselves.

Interestingly enough, Bama started showing Bear's characteristics and mannerisms, like this was divine intervention. We had constant reminders of our recently deceased Bear with the new fluffy white goldendoodle puppy.

And in the end, our new dog exhibits the same traits that Bear reminded us of daily:

Bama is always present.

Bama is always happy (except when the other dogs in our family have his bone).

Bama is always loving.

Bama is loyal.

Bama chases experiences.

Bama greets me every day like it is his first day, and he lives every day like it is his last.

A different dog, but with the same traits as Bear.

Bear brought these six traits to life for me every day.

In seeing my new dog Bama grow, I see these traits in him as well.

These traits are universal in dogs if we pay attention.

They are present in every dog.

Simply, they are the Bear Facts of Life.

Bear taught me so much in the end.

Be present.

Be loving.

Be happy.

Be loyal.

Be chasing life's experience.

Be living life like it is your last day...

because it might be.

Thanks Bear.

For teaching me about life and reminding me how to live a full one.

I cannot wait to see you again, my furry friend.

Be present.

Be loving.

Be happy.

Be loyal.

Be chasing life's
experience.

Be living life like it is
your last day . . .
because it might be.

This was the last picture I ever took of Bear, taken on Tuesday, October 3, 2023, on my 56th Birthday. He died on Sunday, October 8th, five days later.

Acknowledgements

Writing a book is the toughest thing I ever had to do in my life.

It is a lonely endeavor with hurdles of doubt and themes of "who will ever read this" along the way. Throughout this arduous process, one must remember that there is an "audience of one" which was my North Star - my four children whom I wanted to leave these life lessons with through our shared love of this great animal in "Bear" McLaughlin.

To my wife Maria.
To my daughters Payton and Parker.
To my sons, Sean and Ethan.
To my parents, Larry and Gail.
To my brother Robert.
To my sister Colleen.

You encouraged me to get this done. This book does not get done without your constant and never-ending encouragement. Here it is! Thank you. Thank you. Thank you. I love you all!

To Mark and Tricia Wojciechowski who were immediately by our side that tragic day. Thank you from the bottom of our hearts. To our fellow goldendoodle owners and good friends John and Kristen Varner, Jean and Chris Fortune and Buddy and Kathy Russell for being there those tough days after this traumatic event. Thank you for your love and support.

This book's first draft was literally written in thirty minutes as a TEDx talk that (upon the writing of this book) still has not been given. After a few rejections from TEDx, I woke up in the middle of the night and discovered that I just wrote a book. Pure divine intervention. Thank you God!

Maija Lisa Adams and Doug Crowe were

the first to encourage me to get this talk done which is now in written form. Thank you. Maybe one day I will get on the "Red Dot" to get this Ted Talk shared!

Betsy Thorpe, whom I was connected with through my daughter's suitemate at UNC-Chapel Hill, did an incredible job with the content edits. Katherine Bartis did the fine tuning of copy editing and Diana Wade was in charge of the book design. Jill Sullivan, my personal assistant, was there with me every step of the way. Linda Gould, thank you for your last minute proofreading. Thank you to these incredible people for helping this book come to life. It would not have been possible without you!

After Bear's tragedy, I found myself in a few months of mental depression. My wife, kids, parents, brother, sister, extended family, dear friends (especially my Charlotte Catholic high school lifelong friends of Tom Dest,

John Keen, and Steve Grecsek) and patients helped me climb out of these doldrums as did the six life lessons this book continues to remind me of every single day. My therapist, Kim Morris, helped me and encouraged me to get this book done. I cannot thank all of you for your love and care during this tough and vulnerable time. This book is not here without your constant hand holding during this very humbling period of my life. I never experienced mental illness before this event. It is real, and I can acknowledge that I have lived it. It takes a village to help one get out of this valley. I will never ever forget this period of my life and I am sure that those who helped me throughout this won't either. The beauty and by-product of this time is this book. Like a butterfly out of a cocoon, here it is. Thank you to all. The "Phoenix rose!"

Ever since my first pet, Crackers (a beautiful Persian cat), I wanted to be a veterinarian.

I was psyched out to become one due to the competition to get into vet school (one of the few times I balked at "going for it" in life). Throughout pet ownership, I have marveled at this profession and the great veterinarians and their assistants throughout my life. Dr. Marci Godwin and Dr. Julianne Davis-Christ and the extended staff at Mitchell Village Animal Hospital in Morehead City, North Carolina, were there for me and my family throughout this difficult time. They were incredible and had to endure the pain of this event with me and my family. They also assisted with converting the color photos to the black-and-white editions that are used in the black-and-white renditions of the book. Thank you to all of you.

To all of my patients, friends, and family who read rough drafts of this book and made suggestions and recommendations prior to the final version, I cannot thank you enough for your time, love, and encouragement. I hope you are proud of it. Nothing in life is ever accomplished alone. This was a team approach.

To my pets (Bishop, Billabong, and Bama) for being in the writing room every day and at my feet listening to my favorite meditation music of Kip Mazuy. All of you continue to remind me to be present, be loving, be happy, be loyal, chase experiences, and to live each day fully like it is your last.

And of course to Bear. You were my favorite dog. Your memories will be with me forever. I hope that you love this book as much as I did in writing it in your memory.

Thanks for sharing your life lessons with all those who read this book.

I look forward to seeing you again one day my furry friend!

To you, the reader, thank you for taking this journey with me and with Bear.

Always remember that in order to live a fully lived life….Be a Bear and remind yourself daily of "The Bear Facts of Life"!

Patrick McLaughlin

A portion of the proceeds of each book of

The Bear Facts of Life

will be donated to the

Learn more about the author at

Drpatmclaughlin.com.

Books

Group Book Sales

Speaking engagements

Life Alignment Seminars

Life Alignment Online Curriculum

Life Alignment Video Conference Coaching

"A Day on the Dock with Doc"

A full one day life alignment seminar with Dr.
McLaughlin on the same dock that Bear resided.

You only live once...Go for it!

Bear McLaughlin